World Cuisine | **Caribbean Islands**

Caribbean Islands

With recipes by:

Wilo Benet • Mario Pagán • Douglas Rodríguez

World Cuisine

WORLD CUISINE - **Caribbean Islands**

Coordination: ESP Promotions Ltd, London
And TP& Associates, Madrid and Milan

For further information on the collection or to purchase
any books that you have missed, please visit:
www.timesonline.co.uk/cookbooks

For further information regarding publication rights,
please contact: cookbookinfo@gmail.com

Original idea
Jaume Fàbregas

Editorial director
Juan Manuel Bellver

Collection coordinator
Núria Egido

Culinary advisors
Xavier Agulló
R. de Nola
Jorge Osés Labadie

Editors
Mercè Bolló
Pau Raya Castell
Miguel Ángel Sánchez

Contributing editors
Esther Buira
Belén C. Díaz
Patricia Campo
Judit Cusidó
Lola Hernández
M.ª Dolores Escudero
David Ibáñez
Carles Llurda
Meritxell Piqué
Carles Raventós

Photography
Wilo Benet
Christian M. Kempin / Gastrofotos
Daniel Loewe / Joan Jolis, S.L.
Conrado Pastrano

Layout
New Color Book, S.L.

Cover Design
WEP Milano

Pre-print
Digitalscreen

Printers
Avenida Gráfica

ISBN 84-609-7351-4 (complete works)
ISBN 84-609-7370-0 (volume X - Caribbean Islands
Legal deposit: M-39759-2005

Contents

World Cuisine: Caribbean Islands

The first islands that Christopher Columbus set foot on during his discovery of the Americas hundreds of years ago are today perfect examples of how native cuisine has married with, and been influenced by, outside elements. Indigenous products fused with ingredients brought by European colonists, African slaves and, in some cases, combined with oriental elements. The result is a popular cuisine and what it lacks in sophistication, it more than makes up for in colour and flavours.

The Caribbean is today one of the most desirable holiday destinations in the world, thanks to its tropical climate, fertile lands, cultural mix and the survival of ways of life that have almost disappeared in other parts of the world. The region's varied cuisine ranks amongst its attractions. The African and Oriental influences which first appeared in the north of the South American continent are now heavily present in Caribbean cuisine. Caribbean history has been marked by European colonisation, the fundamental role that slaves have played, and the fight for independence, although some islands still remain under the control of North America or European powers. Colonisation has played a huge role in the culinary traditions of the Caribbean; each island's cuisine is based on a combination of indigenous recipes from native tribes, and techniques and ingredients introduced by each colonising nation. Therefore, a notable presence of Spanish, French, Dutch, British and Oriental influences is found; in fact the Caribbean could be thought of as a culinary Tower of Babel. On the other hand, indigenous cuisine and African influence are the main factors that link the cuisines of each Caribbean country.

Indigenous recipes are based on ingredients such as yucca, corn, spicy chillies, wild animal meats and sea produce; fish and seafood are the main source of protein. Amongst local traditions, a process where meat is cooked over intertwined reeds and known as "*barbacoa*" (barbeque) has been common in the Dominican Republic since the pre-Columbian era.

African features

African culinary tradition forms a strong element in Caribbean cooking, and in part can be attributed to the colonisers themselves, thousands of Africans were brought to the islands to work in the new plantations as slaves. The owners of the plantations gave the slaves scarce amounts of rice, cod, beans and meats, and they were forced to use their imagination to produce some of their traditional dishes that we know today. The combination of native tradition, African culture and colonial influences allowed each country to develop its own culinary style known as *cocina criolla* (native cuisine). In Cuba, the national dish is *ajiaco*, which is somewhere between a soup and a stew and contains pork, sweetcorn, sweet potato, yucca, plantain and *salsa criolla* (Creole sauce), made from tomato, onion, garlic and a variety of spices is generously used. Rice is common in many dishes. Rice dishes include Cuban rice, which is made with eggs, plantains, meat and onions; *arroz moros y cristianos* (Moors and Christian rice) or rice with black beans; and Oriental *congrí*, with red beans. The popular meat stew known

as *ropa vieja (*old clothes) contains roasted meat leftovers as well as tomatoes, onions and peppers. Other popular dishes include fish, seafood and green plantain dishes, which are usually fried, eaten as an appetiser or served with meat dishes. In contrast to Cuba, which still remains largely cut off from outside influence, Puerto Rican cuisine has been strongly influenced by North America, although native cuisine survives today thanks to family traditions and state programmes that support traditional restaurants. Some indigenous recipes include *mofongo,* mashed green plantain fried in garlic sauce; *casabe,* pancakes made with yucca flour; *surullos,* cornflour and cheese rolls; stuffed potatoes, which are usually served as a side dish; and *asopao*, a watery rice dish that is served with chicken or fish. In the Dominican Republic, the cuisine and cooking techniques are similar to those of Cuba and Puerto Rico. For instance, the island produces its own version of Cuban *ajiaco* called *sancocho*, a slow-cooked stew, which contains a number of different meats and vegetables. As far as recipes containing corn are concerned, *chenchén,* boiled sweetcorn kernels served with a goat's stew, is extremely popular as is *chacá*, a dessert made with milk, sugar and cinnamon. The Dominican Republic shares its land mass with Haiti, a country with considerable French influence but with scarce resources, meaning that its people have had to survive and adapt limited native ingredients.

Praise for culinary fusion

The culinary fusion and colourful dishes of Caribbean cuisine is most evident on the island of Jamaica. Furthermore, Jamaica's cuisine is one of the spiciest and most seasoned throughout the Caribbean thanks to Oriental influences. *Jerk* sauce is a trademark Jamaican recipe and is made with a mixture of spices, onion, nutmeg or salt, and is used as an accompaniment to meat or fish. Among the most characteristic dishes, *stamp and go,* a cod fritter appetiser made from a tasty seasoned dough, stands out in particular, as well as *sumario,* where meat or fish is cooked in coconut milk and peppers, and *bammy,* a round bread made from yucca. Lastly, to summarise, this brief insight into exotic Caribbean cuisine has enabled an understanding of some of the most characteristic elements of one of the world's most unknown and ignored cuisines: that of African cuisine. Despite its exotic overtones, the intelligent use of indigenous ingredients and a great variety of influences, Caribbean cuisine remains fairly simple, and it is an excellent example of how the native origins of its dishes have influenced present day culinary traditions.

World Cuisine

Starters

This collection of traditional dishes
has been created by:

Estefanía Clemente de la Haza
Restaurant Habana Vieja

Rubén Darío
Restaurant Paladar "El Fausto"

Yilian Pita
Restaurant Tocororo

Ensalada de aguacates
Avocado salad

Level of difficulty: low
Preparation time: 15 minutes

Serves 4
2 ripe avocados
1 onion
Salt
Juice of 1/2 lemon
Olive oil

Carefully peel the avocados and cut into approximately one centimetre-thick slices. Arrange on a plate and season with salt, lemon juice and olive oil. Shred the onions and arrange on top.

Owing to Cuba's climatic and soil conditions, the island is considered a paradise for avocado cultivation, a fruit often eaten in Cuban households. The word *aguacate* (avocado) derives from the word *ahuacatl* from the native tongue of Nahuatl (an American language indigenous to central Mexico). When the Spanish invaded the Aztec and Inca Empires, they discovered that avocados were being cultivated from Mexico to Peru. They christened the fruit "the Indies pear" as its shape and size resembled a Spanish pear.

Ensalada caribeña
Caribbean salad

Serves 4

1/2 iceberg lettuce
1/2 beetroot
2 pineapples
1/2 avocado
1 cucumber
2-3 palm hearts
2 carrots
2 radishes
2 boiled eggs
1 onion
1 tomato
Olives
Balsamic vinegar
Oil
Salt

Wash and chop the lettuce into fine julienne strips and place in the middle of the serving dish or plates. Place the finely sliced carrots, radishes and onion on top of the lettuce. Wash the tomatoes and cut them into medium sized slices. Place them on one side of the plate along with the beetroot and pineapple. Put the cucumber slices on one side and the avocado on the opposite side of the plate. Cut the palm hearts and boiled eggs in slices and place on another side. Scatter the olives.

For the dressing use a vinaigrette made by mixing oil, vinegar and a pinch of salt.

This salad, which is best served fresh, can be adapted according to seasonal variations and personal tastes.

Level of difficulty: low
Preparation time: 15 minutes
Cooking time: 5 minutes

Cóctel de camarones
Prawn cocktail

Serves 4
1kg prawns
2 bay leaves
1/2 lettuce
4 lemon slices
Salt
Pepper
Crushed ice
Mint (to decorate)

For the cocktail sauce:
Ketchup
Mayonnaise
Orange juice
Mustard

Place a pan filled with plenty of water over the heat, when it starts to boil add the prawns (already peeled and cleaned), bay leaves, salt and pepper. Leave to cook for five minutes, drain them and put to one side to allow to cool. Crush some ice cubes and place along the bottom of four cocktail glasses. Place a layer of washed and finely chopped lettuce on top of the ice and then on top of the lettuce place a layer of prawns mixed with cocktail sauce – previously made by mixing all of the ingredients together in quantities according to the diners' tastes. Decorate the glasses with lemon slices and a sprig of mint.

Prawn cocktail must always be served very cold. In Cuba there is no difference between the prawn and the shrimp, unlike in England.

Level of difficulty: medium
Preparation time: 1 hour
Cooking time: 1 hour

Tamal en su hoja
Tamales wrapped in corn husks

Serves 4 *(8 tamales)*
8 corn husks
3 cups ground maize or white cornmeal
1 cup water
500g shredded pork
3 garlic cloves finely chopped
1 onion finely chopped
1 red pepper finely chopped
1/2 cup tomato purée
1/2 cup dry white wine
Salt
Pepper

Combine the ground maize and the water in a bowl. After three or four minutes, drain. Fry the pork and remove from the frying pan. In the meat fat, fry the garlic, onion, finely chopped pepper, tomato purée and wine. When the onion and pepper are soft and translucent, add the soaked ground maize and fried meat. Season. Place this mixture into the centre of a corn husk, roll up, fold and secure with cocktail sticks. Simmer the *tamales* in water for approximately one hour.

The word *tamal* is derived from the Nahuatl word *tamalli*. This boiled or steamed snack can be wrapped in corn husks or banana leaves. The meat and corn mixture may also be cooked in moulds.

Level of difficulty: medium
Preparation time: 1 hour
Cooking time: 1 hour

Saladitos
Nibbles

Serves 4
200g gouda cheese
1 tablespoon cornflour
50g butter
250g minced veal
1 red pepper
2 garlic cloves
12 prawns
Flour
Breadcrumbs
Lemon

Finely grate the gouda cheese and mix with the cornflour and softened butter to form a consistent paste.

Separately mix the meat with the finely chopped red pepper, garlic and a few breadcrumbs. Lastly, remove the heads and shells from the prawns, keeping the legs. Cover in flour and fry in plenty of oil until they are crispy.

Roll the cheese paste into little balls, fry in plenty of oil and place on absorbent paper. Also form little balls with the meat mixture and repeat the above procedure. Place the fried food on the plates and decorate with a slice of lemon.

These snacks are ideal as a starter to any Caribbean meal.

Level of difficulty: low
Preparation time: 35 minutes
Cooking time: 25 minutes

Fufú de plátano
Plantain purée

Serves 4
2 green plantains
2 semi-ripe plantains
250g lean pork, diced
1 egg
Salt

Peel the plantains and chop roughly. Boil a pan of water and add the green plantain chunks. After approximately fifteen minutes, add the semi-ripe plantain. While the plantains are cooking, fry the pork in its own fat and sprinkle with salt. When tender, add to the drained plantains and mix with one egg. Mash whilst hot until smooth. This dish can be eaten as a starter or served as a side dish.

A simple dish of boiled and mashed banana was often given to African slaves in Cuba during English rule. It is said that English traders used to shout "food, food!" when rations were distributed, lending the name "fufú" to the dish. *Fufu* is eaten on other Caribbean islands, yet under different names: *mofongo* in Puerto Rico, *mangú* in the Dominican Republic, *matajíbaro,* etc.

Level of difficulty: medium
Preparation time: 35 minutes
Cooking time: 20 minutes

Machuquillo
Plantain and pork fritters

Serves 4

3 green plantains
150g crispy pork crackling
2 eggs
Salt
Oil

Peel the plantains and cut into roughly three-centimetre slices. Fry in plenty of oil at low heat until the fruit has cooked sufficiently. When soft, use a flat utensil to flatten the plantains (plate, spatula etc.). Return to the frying pan, increase the heat to high heat, and fry in plenty of oil until crisp and golden. Remove from the pan and place onto absorbent paper to drain the excess fat. Pulse in a blender with the pork crackling and eggs. When smooth, season with salt and shape into small fritters using a spoon. Fry in very hot oil until golden.

These banana and pork fritters may be served as an appetiser or as a side dish to accompany any meat or fish dish. Pork cutlets served with *machuquillo* are extremely popular in Cuba.

Tostones rellenos de camarones
Fried plantains stuffed with prawns

Level of difficulty: medium
Preparation time: 50 minutes
Cooking time: 25 minutes

Serves 4
3 green plantains

For the prawn filling:
400g prawns
2 garlic cloves
1/2 onion
1/2 red pepper
1 sprig parsley
1/2 cup tomato sauce
1/2 cup white wine
1/2 teaspoon Worcestershire sauce
1 bay leaf
Oil
Salt
Pepper

First, prepare the prawn stuffing (see *Sautéed prawns*, p.68). To prepare the fried plantains, peel and cut into roughly three-centimetre pieces. Fry in plenty of oil until golden. Now place on absorbent kitchen paper to remove the excess fat. When cool, shape into little tartlets and return to the frying pan. Fry for a further three minutes until crispy. Finally, stuff the fried plantains with the prawn filling. Serve immediately.

Plantains must be fried with great care. The oil must be extremely hot to ensure that the plantain does not break up during frying. Other typical Caribbean fillings include crabmeat, lobster, *salmorejo de jueyes* (crabmeat stew), a combination of chicken and ham, or mincemeat.

Level of difficulty: low
Preparation time: 25 minutes
Cooking time: 20 minutes

Maduros fritos
Fried ripe bananas

Serves 4
3 ripe plantain bananas
Oil

Peel the ripe bananas and chop them into slices. Fry them in a frying pan or deep-fat fryer with plenty of oil. Place them on absorbent paper to collect the excess oil and serve as a starter or side dish to a meal such as roasted meat or white rice.

This dish can be made with any type of bananas. It is also delicious with bananas from the Canary Islands, although it is recommended that they are not too ripe as otherwise they will soak up too much oil.

Level of difficulty: low
Preparation time: 10 minutes
Cooking time: 30 minutes

Yuca con mojo
Yucca in garlic sauce

Serves 4
3-4 yuccas
Salt

For the sauce:
Juice of 1-2 bitter oranges
Olive oil
3 garlic cloves, crushed

Peel the yucca and cut into roughly five-centimetre chunks. Boil in salted water over a medium heat for thirty minutes, until soft. Meanwhile, prepare the sauce. Mix the bitter orange juice with the crushed garlic cloves and olive oil. When the yucca is soft, drain and arrange in a dish or onto individual serving plates. Drizzle with the sauce whilst still hot.

This sauce is normally made with bitter orange juice, but lemon juice may be used instead. If desired, add onion rings to enhance the flavour of the sauce.

Level of difficulty: low
Preparation time: 20 minutes
Cooking time: 45 minutes

Frijoles negros
Black beans

Serves 4
*500g black beans (*frijoles*)*
1 medium sized onion
1 green pepper
1 bay leaf
1 garlic bulb
1 pinch ground cumin
1 teaspoon oregano
Olive oil
Salt

Soak the beans in water overnight. Now place into a saucepan, cover with water and boil until soft. Meanwhile, finely chop the garlic, onion and pepper. Fry in oil with a pinch of ground cumin and the oregano until golden. When the beans are cooked, ladle off a little water if necessary and add the onion and pepper mixture. With a large spoon, crush as many beans as necessary to form a thick sauce. Just before serving, drizzle with a dash of oil.

This basic traditional recipe is eaten daily in Cuban households. *Frijoles* are never absent from the dinner table at Christmas time.

Level of difficulty: low
Preparation time: 25 minutes
Cooking time: 1 hour

Moros y cristianos
Rice with black beans

Serves 4
2 cups black beans
5 cups water
3 cups long-grain rice
1/2 garlic bulb
1 bay leaf
1/2 teaspoon ground cumin
Olive oil
Salt

Soak the beans overnight in plenty of water. Now place two cups of black beans and five cups of water in a saucepan (or use a pressure cooker for speed) and cook over a moderate heat until soft. Now crush the garlic and fry in oil in a saucepan along with the bay leaf and a pinch of ground cumin. When the garlic is soft, add the beans, the bean cooking stock and three cups of rice. Add salt and leave to cook over a very low heat for about twenty-five to thirty minutes. When the rice is cooked, stir to separate the grains. Cover the pan until ready to serve.

Although many people confuse the two, it is important to make the distinction between *arroz moros y cristianos* (rice with black beans) and *arroz congrí* (rice with red beans). If making *arroz congrí,* a dish eaten in Haiti, Puerto Rico, Dominican Republic and other Caribbean islands, only the beans need to be substituted.

Level of difficulty: low
Preparation time: 20 minutes
Cooking time: 30 minutes

Arroz frito
Fried rice

Serves 4

2.5 cups long-grain rice
4 cups water
50g ham (or fat bacon)
50g smoked pork loin
4 eggs
4 leeks
Soy sauce
Oil

Heat the rice in a pan full of water. Add a dash of oil. While the rice is cooking, slice the ham and pork loin into roughly three-centimetre fine strips. Sauté in a frying pan with a little oil. Clean and slice the leeks. Steam until tender, set aside. Prepare an omelette with the eggs and cut into fine strips. When the rice is cooked, add a little soy sauce (to give it a touch of colour). Add the strips of ham, pork and omelette. Sauté for a couple of minutes, stirring until the ingredients are combined. Just before serving, add the sliced leek and toss.

Long-grain rice is used to make steamed rice. The seeds of the rice plant are first milled to remove the outer husks; if the process is continued, white rice is obtained.

Level of difficulty: low
Preparation time: 30 minutes
Cooking time: 20 minutes

Arroz con huevos
Cuban rice

Serves 4
8 eggs
250g rice
2 avocados
4 ripe plantains
Salt

For the tomato sauce:
1 large onion, finely chopped
3 tbs oil
10 tomatoes, deseeded and chopped
Salt and pepper
Pinch of sugar
1/2 pint chicken stock

Cook the rice in salted water for twenty minutes. Drain and set aside.

To make the tomato sauce cook the onion in the oil until transparent. Add the tomatoes, salt, pepper and sugar. Cook slowly for 25 minutes. Add the stock and cook for a further 5 minutes. Liquidise the sauce and sieve. If too thin, boil until thickened, taking care it doesn't stick.

Meanwhile, fry the eggs in a frying pan (two per person) and place onto absorbent paper to remove the excess fat. Peel the plantains and cut each fruit into three pieces. Fry in oil. Peel the avocados and cut into segments. When prepared, serve the eggs with the white rice, tomato sauce, fried bananas and avocado.

The name of this dish (*Cuban rice*) is actually Spanish. In Cuba, the dish is called *rice with eggs*.

Level of difficulty: low
Preparation time: 20 minutes
Cooking time: 45 minutes

Arroz con pollo
Chicken with rice

Serves 4

1.5 kg chicken (skin removed and diced).
2.5 cups long-grain rice
200g fresh chopped tomatoes (skin removed)
1 onion
1 green pepper
1/2 bulb garlic
2 small bottles of beer
Roasted red peppers
Oil
Salt

Finely chop the onion, garlic and pepper, or pulse in a blender. Fry in a little oil in a saucepan with a pinch of salt and the chicken. When the vegetables and meat are tender, add the chopped tomatoes and continue frying. Now add the rice and the two bottles of beer. Cover and leave to cook over a low heat for thirty minutes. Before serving, garnish with the strips of roasted red pepper.

If preparing *arroz a la chorrera* (rice soaked in beer), also a typical Cuban dish, add more beer so that the rice is more liquid, literally "*chorreando*" (soaking).

World Cuisine

Main courses

Level of difficulty: medium
Preparation time: 20 minutes
Cooking time: 40 minutes

Ropa vieja
Shredded veal in sauce

Serves 4
500g veal
2 green peppers
2 onions
1 bay leaf
1/2 bulb garlic
1 pinch ground cumin
150g chopped tomatoes
Oil
Salt

Remove the fat and sinews from the meat, dice into roughly four centimetre pieces (cutting across the meat sinews to facilitate shredding). Boil in water with the bay leaf until tender. Leave to cool. Meanwhile, wash the peppers and cut into fine strips. Peel the onion and slice. Crush the garlic and lightly fry in oil with the strips of pepper, onion slices, chopped tomatoes and a pinch of cumin.

Once the meat has cooled, shred and add to the pan. Cover everything in the pan with the cooking stock and leave to cook until nearly all the water has evaporated. Do not allow to dry out.

This is possibly the most internationally known Cuban dish. It is named *ropa vieja (old clothes)* because generally, it is made with the leftover meat, used for making bean soup.

Level of difficulty: low
Preparation time: 25 minutes
Cooking time: 50 minutes

Guiso de maíz
Sweetcorn stew

Serves 4
4 corn on the cob
1 smoked pork cutlet
500g fried pork chunks
150g pumpkin
150g malanga *(tuber resembling sweet potato)*
6 tomatoes
1 onion
1 bulb garlic
1 green pepper
Oil
Salt

Firstly, chop the onion, garlic and pepper finely. Sauté in a pan in a little oil. Add the chopped tomatoes. Meanwhile, fry the diced pork until tender in another pan. Remove the corn from the cobs and cook in boiling water with the *malanga* that has been cut into approximately one centimetre-thick slices. When the sweetcorn and *malanga* are semi-cooked, add the meat, tomatoes, onion, garlic and pepper mixture to the saucepan. Add the cubed pumpkin last as this softens quickly. Leave to cook until the mixture thickens. Serve with white rice (see *White rice,* p.52).

There are several versions of this typical Cuban stew, including recipes with ham, *chorizo* sausage and other meats; the stew may also be seasoned with pepper, oregano, cumin and other spices.

Level of difficulty: high
Preparation time: 40 minutes
Cooking time: 1 hour 30 minutes

Sancocho de siete carnes
Seven meat *sancocho*

Serves 4

200g goat meat (or lamb)
200g longaniza *mildly-spiced pork sausage (or Italian mild sausage)*
200g pork
200g smoked ham bones
350g beef (with bones)
400g chicken
400g pork cutlets
2 lemons
1 tablespoon chopped garlic
2 large green chilli peppers
100g yucca
100g yam
100g yautia (malanga, *similar to sweet potato)*
2 green plantains – 1 chopped into 2 1/2 cm pieces, 1 grated
1 meat stock cube
2 potatoes
2 corn on the cobs (optional)
1 celery stick
1/2 teaspoon oregano
1/2 teaspoon coriander
2 teaspoons vinegar
Bitter oranges (Agrio de naranja) *or spicy sauce*
Oil
Salt

Dice the meat and cover with lemon juice. Heat some oil in a saucepan and lightly fry the beef, oregano, coriander, chopped garlic, chillies and vinegar. Add a pinch of salt. Cover the pan and stir occasionally. Add a little water to prevent the meat sticking to the base of the pan. After twenty minutes, add the pork and lightly fry for about ten to fifteen minutes. When brown, add all the remaining meats and the crumbled stock cube. Leave to cook over a low heat for about ten minutes, adding a little water if the mixture starts to look dry.

Now cover the ingredients with water and bring to the boil. Add the peeled yam, *yautia*, yucca and one plantain, diced into roughly 21/2 centimetre pieces. Leave to boil for ten minutes and then add the other plantain that has been grated. Peel and chop the potatoes. Add to the mixture along with the chopped celery, and if desired, the corns on the cob cut into approximately five centimetre chunks.

Add bitter orange sauce to taste (or another spicy sauce), normally about two tablespoonfuls, and water (as much as the stew needs). Leave to simmer until the stew is cooked, season with salt and serve hot.

> This traditional Dominican dish is usually served with white rice and avocado.

Level of difficulty: low
Preparation time: 20 minutes
Cooking time: 4 hours

Pierna asada
Roasted leg of pork

Serves 4
1 leg of pork
2 bay leaves
1 tablespoon oregano
1 bulb of garlic
Juice of 6-8 lemons
Salt
Oil

Place the whole leg of pork on an oven tray. Make cuts in the meat with a sharp knife so that the meat soaks up the sauce. In a bowl, mix together the lemon juice, crushed garlic, tablespoonful of oregano and a couple of bay leaves. Mix the sauce with oil and pour over the leg of pork. Place the meat in the oven at a low temperature and leave to cook for between four and five hours. Serve the meat in slices in its juices and with white rice (see *White rice,* p.52).

Roasted leg of pork is one of the most popular dishes in Cuba. It is also very typical to serve it with potato purée.

Level of difficulty: low
Preparation time: 20 minutes
Cooking time: 50 minutes

Fricasé de pollo
Chicken stew

Serves 4

1.5kg chicken, cut into eight pieces
1 large onion
1 green pepper
4 ripe tomatoes
1/2 bulb garlic
Green olives
2 tablespoons dry white wine
3 small bottles of beer
Oil
Salt

For the white rice:
2 cups rice
2 cups water
3 tablespoons olive oil
Salt

For the white rice: Heat the rice, water, oil and a pinch of salt in a pan over a very low flame. Stir gently and cover. Do not remove the lid for twenty-five minutes. When the rice is cooked, stir with a fork to separate the grains. Cover again until ready for serving.

Chop the tomatoes, onion, garlic and pepper and lightly fry in oil over a low heat. Season with a pinch of salt. When softened, add the pieces of chicken. Stir well to impregnate the meat with the other ingredients. Now add the beer and wine. After about ten to fifteen minutes, add the olives. Leave for another ten minutes over the heat and serve with the white rice.

When making this dish, it is very important that the sauce thickens a little. The stew must be left over a very low heat until the stock has practically evaporated.

Level of difficulty: low
Preparation time: 40 minutes
Cooking time: 1 hour 30 minutes

Tasajo
Dried salted meat

Serves 4

2-2.5kg horse meat (to be shredded), or can use beef
2 green peppers
3 onions
1 bulb of garlic
125g fresh chopped tomatoes
Oil
Salt

First, dry the pieces of meat. Cover the bottom of a baking tray with a thick layer of salt. Place the meat on top and cover the meat with another layer of salt. Leave to stand for ten days in a dry cool place. When ready, wash the pieces of meat in water, dry well and cube into four centimetre pieces. Boil for three to four hours, changing the cooking water a couple of times, until tender. Reserve the stock.

When tender, remove from the pan, leave to cool and shred with a fork or by hand. Now finely slice the onions and peppers, and finely chop the garlic. Mix with the chopped tomatoes and a little oil. When well mixed, add the shredded meat and some of the meat stock to the pan. Cook until the meat is succulent, or for about thirty minutes. The meat may be served with white rice or roasted sweet potato.

When boiling the meat after drying, it is advisable to change the cooking water at least twice. *Tasajo* can be made with different types of meat: beef, smoked pork, chicken...

Level of difficulty: low
Preparation time: 20 minutes
Cooking time: 30 minutes

Masas fritas
Fried pork cubes

Serves 4
800g lean pork
1/2 bulb garlic
Juice of 4 lemons
2 bay leaves
Fresh oregano
Pepper
Salt
Oil

Cut the pork into cubes and season well. Place in a pan with the lemon juice, crushed garlic, two bay leaves and a little fresh oregano and cook until the meat is tender and nearly all of the liquid has evaporated. Now fry the meat in hot oil (180°C) until golden and crispy. Serve with salad.

Fried plantains and *machuquillo* plantain mash are often used to accompany this simple meal.

Level of difficulty: low
Preparation time: 45 minutes
Cooking time: 45 minutes

Carne con papas
Meat and potato stew

Serves 6-8

1kg veal
1kg potatoes
1 onion chopped
1 pepper chopped
3 garlic cloves crushed
1 cup of tomato sauce (see p.38)
1 cup of dry wine
1 cup of water
*1 cup of "alcaparrado" (olives
with capers in a jar)*
1 tomato
1 teaspoon salt
1 teaspoon paprika
1/2 teaspoon pepper
1 bay leaf
1/2 cup olive oil

Cut the meat into small dice and fry in a saucepan with oil. When slightly brown, season with salt, paprika, pepper and the bay leaf. Add the chopped onion and pepper as well as the crushed garlic.

When everything is browned, add the tomato sauce and dry wine. Cover with the cup of water. Place over a medium heat for about twenty-five minutes. Half way through the cooking, add the diced potatoes and "alcaparrado". When the potatoes are soft, serve the hot stew.

This Cuban stew can also be made with pork. The word "*alcaparrado*" which in Spanish means a type of olive that is sold with capers and sometimes pieces of red pepper, is simply referred to in Cuba as "*alcaparras en conserva*" (tinned capers).

Level of difficulty: low
Preparation time: 25 minutes
Cooking time: 1 hour

Vaca frita
Fried beef

Serves 4

*500g beef (boneless flank or
breast)
1/2 onion sliced
1/2 green pepper sliced
2 garlic cloves sliced
1 bay leaf
1/2 teaspoon cumin
1/2 teaspoon oregano
1 meat stock cube
Olive oil
Salt
Pepper*

For the garnish:
*4 medium sized potatoes
1/2 lettuce
1 tomato
1 cucumber
1 onion
Red cabbage*

Cook the meat with the onion, green pepper, garlic, bay leaves, spices and stock cube in plenty of water for an hour. Remove the meat from the pan and cut into pieces of about ten centimetres. Flatten them with a pestle until the threads are separated.

Chop the potatoes and fry in plenty of oil. Prepare a side salad with lettuce, red cabbage, cucumber and tomato. Cut the remaining onion into rings and blanch in boiling water. Season the threads of meat and place them on the grill. Once they are hot, place them on the plate and decorate with the garnish.

This stew is very similar to "*ropa vieja*" (old clothes). The main difference is that Fried Beef is cooked on the grill. Instead of flattening the meat with a pestle, you can strip the pieces of meat by hand or using a fork.

Costillas de cerdo con arroz moros y cristianos
Pork chops with Moors and Christians rice

Level of difficulty: medium
Preparation time: 30 minutes
Cooking time: 25 minutes

Serves 4
1.5kg pork chops
3 garlic cloves finely chopped
1 teaspoon salt
1/2 bitter orange
1 onion cut into rings
Olive oil
Salt

For the rice:
200g black beans
200g steamed rice
1 onion
1 bay leaf
2 garlic cloves
Oregano

Remove the fat from the pork chops. Sprinkle the finely chopped garlic cloves and salt over the meat and baste with the bitter orange juice. Place the onion rings over the top and leave the chops to marinade for one hour. Once this time has passed, drain the meat and fry in a frying pan with oil until golden brown.

Make the *congrí* rice (see *Moros y Cristianos* – Rice with black beans: See p.34) and serve as a garnish for the chops.

The pork chops can be served with the famous *congrí* rice or with white rice a healthier option that makes up for all the fat that will be eaten from the meat.

Level of difficulty: medium
Preparation time: 40 minutes
Cooking time: 1 hour

Chenchén con chivo guisado
Chenchén with goat stew

Serves 4
For the *chenchén*:
1kg sweetcorn kernels
2l milk
200g butter
4 tablespoons oil
1 tablespoon aniseed powder
Salt

For the goat meat:
600g goat meat, diced
1 garlic clove chopped
1 onion chopped
2 green chillies chopped
1 glass rum (or whisky or white wine)
Oil
Salt
Pepper

To make the *chenchén*: Wash the sweetcorn in plenty of water and leave to soak for forty-five minutes. Drain well and place in a pan with the milk, butter, oil and tablespoon of aniseed. Heat and stir continuously until the mixture thickens to the desired consistency. Now cover the pan and leave to cook over a medium heat for fifteen to twenty minutes. Add salt to taste and leave to stand.

Heat some oil in a frying pan. Lightly fry the finely chopped onion, garlic and chillies. When they start to brown, add the diced meat. When the meat is semi-cooked, add the rum. Continue stirring until the alcohol has evaporated. Leave over a medium heat until the meat is tender and succulent. Arrange the goat meat on plates, drizzle with the meat juices and serve with the *chenchén*.

Chenchén is a typical dish from the south of the Dominican Republic.

Level of difficulty: low
Preparation time: 20 minutes
Cooking time: 25 minutes

Mar y tierra
Land and sea

Serves 4
600g lamb, diced
200g prawns, peeled
2 glasses white wine
Salt

For the Creole sauce:
200g fresh chopped tomatoes
1 onion finely chopped
2 garlic cloves finely chopped
1 glass white wine
1 bay leaf
1 teaspoon sugar
3 teaspoons salt
Oil
Pepper
Salt

For the white rice:
2 cups long-grain rice (or basmati)
2 cups water
3 tablespoons olive oil
Salt

First, prepare the Creole sauce. Heat a little oil in a frying pan. Add the chopped tomatoes, finely chopped onion, garlic and a glass of white wine. When slightly reduced, add the bay leaf, a teaspoon of sugar, three teaspoons of salt and a little pepper. When the sauce starts to thicken, remove from the heat and leave to stand.

Now heat some oil in another frying pan. Brown the lamb. When almost cooked, add the peeled prawns. Cook for about five minutes before adding the white wine. When the alcohol has evaporated, add the Creole sauce and leave to cook for a further ten to fifteen minutes. Serve with white rice.

For the white rice: Cook the rice, water, a little oil and salt over a very low heat. Stir gently and then cover. Do not remove the lid for twenty-five minutes. When the rice is cooked, stir with a fork to separate the grains.

Cover again until ready for serving.

This dish combines sea and land flavours to perfection. Chicken may be used instead of lamb for equally excellent results.

Level of difficulty: low
Preparation time: 40 minutes
Cooking time: 15 minutes

Enchilada de camarones
Sautéed prawns

Serves 6
1 kg prawns
1 onion chopped
3 garlic cloves crushed
1 red pepper chopped
1 cup tomato sauce (see p.38)
1/2 cup white wine
2 bay leaves
1 teaspoon Worcestershire sauce
1/2 cup olive oil
Salt
Pepper

First peel and wash the prawns. Now fry in very hot oil. When they start to colour, add the chopped onion and pepper, and the crushed garlic. Lightly fry. When cooked, add the tomato sauce, bay leaf, wine, Worcestershire sauce, salt and pepper. Continue frying over a low heat for fifteen minutes. The *enchilada* may be served on its own or with white rice, lettuce and tomato.

Although Europeans often associate *enchilada* with spiciness, Cubans consider an *enchilada* to be any dish that is seasoned, but not to excess.

Level of difficulty: low
Preparation time: 15 minutes
Cooking time: 20 minutes

Pargo con salsa Jerk
Jerk snapper

Serves 4

4 snappers

For the *Jerk* sauce:
6-8 garlic cloves
6 spring onions
1/2 cup brown sugar
4 chilli peppers (Havana chillies)
1 tablespoon cayenne pepper
1 tablespoon chopped thyme
1 teaspoon cinnamon
1/2 teaspoon nutmeg
Soy sauce
Salt
Pepper

First prepare the *jerk* sauce. Place all of the ingredients in a bowl or food processor and blend until smooth. The sauce may be kept in the fridge for weeks. To enhance its flavour, add more cayenne pepper or hot chilli powder.

To prepare the fish, coat well with the *jerk* sauce and marinate for at least two hours in the fridge so that the fish infuses with the flavours. Then, place in an oven dish and cover with aluminium foil. Bake until cooked.

Jerk sauce is a basic part of Jamaican cookery and is used in meat and fish marinades. The food is then traditionally cooked on the barbecue and flavoured by adding thyme and other herbs to the charcoal.

Level of difficulty: low
Preparation time: 40 minutes
Cooking time: 15 minutes

Langosta enchilada
Lobster stew

Serves 4

4 lobsters
16 clams
1/2 onion finely chopped
2 garlic cloves finely chopped
1/2 red pepper
1/2 cup of tomato sauce (see p.38)
1/2 cup of white wine
1 bay leaf
1/2 teaspoon Worcestershire sauce
1/2 cup olive oil
Parsley finely chopped
Salt
Pepper

For the white rice:
2 cups of long grained rice (optionally basmati)
2 cups of water
3 tablespoons olive oil
Salt

Remove the tails from the lobsters. Wash and chop the meat into approximately five centimetre pieces keeping the shells on to make a tastier stew. Place the rice, water, a little oil and salt into a pan over a very low heat. Lightly stir and then cover. Keep covered for twenty-five minutes. When the rice is cooked, stir with a fork to separate the grains. Cover again until ready for serving.

Fry the lobster pieces in very hot oil. When they start to turn pink, add the finely chopped onion and pepper and crushed garlic.

Leave to cook together for a few minutes and then add the finely chopped parsley, tomato sauce, bay leaf, wine, Worcestershire sauce. Season to taste.

Keep over a low heat for about fifteen minutes. Add the heads if you wish to use them for presentation. Five minutes before the cooking has finished, add the clams.

Serve with white rice and salad.

It is advisable to cook the lobster in its shell to enhance its taste and make the stew more succulent. To remove the shell from the lobster and to keep the meat intact, hit it with a large knife.

Level of difficulty: low
Preparation time: 20 minutes
Cooking time: 20 minutes

Camarón termidor
Prawn thermidor

Serves 4
400g prawns
150g sliced mushrooms
100ml cream
1 glass white wine
1 tablespoon butter
Grated cheese (optional)
Salt

Melt the butter in a frying pan. Add the peeled prawns, chopped mushrooms, cream, white wine and a pinch of salt, all at the same time. Leave to cook over a low heat until the mushrooms and prawns are soft and the sauce has thickened a little then add the grated cheese.

Serve very hot.

The name of this dish, which is also excellent with lobster, comes from the month of heat (thermidor or *termidor* in Spanish), the eleventh month of the French Republican Calendar (from 19th July to 17th August). Trotsky reinterpreted the term and used it to mean the gaining of power for Stalinist conservative bureaucracy.

World Cuisine

Desserts

Level of difficulty: low
Preparation time: 15 minutes
Cooking time: 40 minutes

Dulce de papaya
Papaya *delice*

Serves 4
350g papaya
150g sugar
Lemon rind
Cream cheese
1 cinnamon stick
1 pinch salt

Peel the papaya and dice. Place a saucepan on the heat and add the papaya and sugar. Cover with water. Add a pinch of salt, the cinnamon stick and lemon rind to flavour. Leave to cook over a low heat until the papaya becomes a thick sauce. Serve cold with cream cheese. Remove the cinnamon stick and lemon rind before serving.

A pinch of salt is added to many Cuban desserts.

Level of difficulty: low
Preparation time: 35 minutes
Cooking time: 40 minutes

Coco rallado
Grated coconut

Serves 4
250g dried coconut
Cream cheese
100g sugar
100ml water
1 pinch salt
Rind of 1/2 lemon grated

Crack open the coconut (mature brown variety). Cut out the flesh and grate with a *guayo* or a grater. Now heat the grated coconut, water, sugar and a pinch of salt in a saucepan. Leave to cook until almost all the liquid has evaporated. Now add the lemon rind to add flavour. When the coconut forms a thick paste, remove from the heat and leave to cool. Serve with cream cheese.

A *guayo* is a grater used by indigenous Indians to make yucca bread.

Level of difficulty: low
Preparation time: 25 minutes
Cooking time: 2 hours

Flan habanero
Condensed milk pudding

Serves 4
6 eggs
1 tin condensed milk (400g)
Water

For the caramel:
Caster Sugar

To make the caramel: First fill a sink with 3-4" cold water. Next put the caster sugar into a clean pan with a very little water. Heat slowly until the sugar dissolves then boil rapidly until mid brown. Be careful it burns very easily. When an even colour, plunge base of the pan into the cold water to stop it cooking. Set aside.

Beat the eggs and mix with the condensed milk. Fill the empty condensed milk tin with water and add to the mixture. Mix thoroughly. Coat a jelly mould (or individual ramekins) with caramel. Now pour in the egg and milk mixture. Cover with foil and seal well to avoid any water entering. Cook in a bain-marie (roasting tin with 1" water in the bottom) for a couple of hours. Leave to cool before placing into the fridge.

As its name suggests, this is a typical dessert from Havana and is extremely sweet due the quantity of condensed milk used.

Torrejas
Sweet fried bread in milk and wine

Level of difficulty: low
Preparation time: 25 minutes
Cooking time: 15 minutes

Serves 4

12 slices of baguette
3 eggs
1l milk
1 cinnamon stick
Dry white wine
Soya oil (for frying)
Sugar
Water

Place the milk and cinnamon stick in a pan and bring to the boil. Arrange the slices of bread (preferably dried) in a large serving dish and pour over the boiled milk and cinnamon mixture. Now pour a tablespoon of dry white wine onto each individual slice of bread, cover the serving dish with a cloth and leave to stand for twenty-four hours.

Now beat the eggs, carefully dip the bread slices in the beaten egg and fry in very hot oil until golden. Place onto absorbent kitchen paper to remove any excess fat. Meanwhile, prepare a sugar and water syrup in a pan. Drizzle the bread slices with the syrup just before serving.

The sweet fried bread may also be drizzled with good quality cane sugar honey.

Level of difficulty: medium
Preparation time: 25 minutes
Cooking time: 50 minutes

Pudin de guayaba
Guava pudding

Serves 4

1 loaf of dry bread, without the
crusts
6 eggs
4 pieces of guava
1 can condensed milk (400g)
Water
Liquid caramel (see p.82)

For the pieces of guava:
250g ripe or semi-ripe guavas
200ml water
1 cup of sugar
1 cinnamon stick
1 pinch salt

First make the caramel and coat the mould with it. Set aside. Peel the guavas and cut in two. Carefully remove the seeds and discard. Cook the shells in plenty of water until semi-soft. Ladle out 200ml of liquid from the cooking water and transfer into a saucepan with the sugar, cinnamon stick, pinch of salt and the semi-cooked guava shells. Heat over a low heat until a syrup has formed. Leave the mixture to cool before placing in the fridge.

Cut the bread into fine slices. Beat the eggs in a bowl and mix with the condensed milk. Fill the empty condensed milk can with water to get the exact measurement and add to the mixture.

Stir and then add the small pieces of guava along with the bread. Mix together and pour into a mould that you have previously spread with caramel. Leave to stand for at least one hour so that the bread soaks up the mixture and then cook the pudding in a Bain Marie (roasting tin with 1" water in the bottom) in the oven. Check to see if it is ready by inserting a skewer in the middle of the pudding – if it is dry and clean, the pudding is ready. Remove from the heat, leave to cool and place in the fridge until ready for serving.

If preferred, you can make the caramel by melting sugar with water in the mould or a pan. The proportion is two tablespoons of water per three of sugar.

Level of difficulty: medium
Preparation time: 25 minutes
Cooking time: 50 minutes

Pudin de coco
Coconut pudding

Serves 4

1 loaf of dry bread, without the crusts
6 eggs
100-150g grated coconut
1 can condensed milk (400g)
Water
Liquid caramel (see p.82)

Make the caramel. Spread the mould with a layer of caramel.

Mix the eggs with the can of condensed milk and the same amount of water (you can use the empty condensed milk can to get the exact quantity) and beat together.

When the liquid is well beaten, add the grated coconut and finely sliced bread. Knead the paste and pour into a mould that you have previously spread with caramel.

Leave to stand for at least one hour so that the bread soaks up the mixture and then cook the pudding in a Bain Marie (roasting tin with 1" water in the bottom) in the oven.

Check that it is cooked by using a skewer, remove from the heat, leave to cool and place in the fridge until ready for serving.

Coconut is one of the star products in Cuban cooking and it is used in many recipes, varying from sweet to salty dishes.

Authors' selection

Wilo Benet
Pikayo Restaurant
(San Juan)

Having trained at the Culinary Institute of America and in prestigious establishments such as The Maurice restaurant, The Water Club and Le Bernardin in New York, Benet returned to Puerto Rico in 1988 to work as chef at the Governor's Mansion. Two years later, he opened Pikayo, where he creates imaginative dishes of contemporary Puerto Rican cooking.

Mario Pagán
Chayote Restaurant
(San Juan)

A Puerto Rican lover of Caribbean gastronomy, Mario Pagán masterfully combines ingredients into surprising concoctions, fusing traditional and contemporary cuisine. Trained at the prestigious Johnson and Wales University of Culinary Arts, he continued his professional career with Alfredo Ayala, founder of Chayote restaurant. Mario Pagán is now the owner and chef at Chayote, and creates superb Caribbean cuisine.

Douglas Rodríguez
Ola Restaurant
(Miami)

Having trained in prestigious hotels in Miami, Rodríguez is now considered a representative of contemporary Latin cuisine. Since opening Yuca restaurant in 1989, he has won numerous awards including Miami Chef Of The Year when he was 24 years old, part of Chefs of America. *Newsweek* have named him among the top one hundred Americans who will be most influential in the new millennium. He is currently working at Ola restaurant with innovative pastry chef José Luis Flores.

Raviolis rellenos de pesto y trufa negra
Ravioli filled with pesto and black truffle

Wilo Benet

Serves 4
60g foie gras
8 wonton *wrappers*
2 black truffle cheeses
16 spinach leaves
6 tablespoons pine nuts
4 morel mushrooms
12 tarragon leaves
2 beaten eggs
2 tablespoons white truffle oil
Olive oil
Flour
Salt
Pepper

Make the pesto with the boiled spinach and pine nuts by blending them together. Season. Add olive oil until the desired consistency has been obtained. Set aside for the filling.

Dice the truffle cheeses and set aside. Now lay out the *wonton* wrappers on a work surface, sprinkle with a little flour. Place half a teaspoon of pesto sauce and a little truffle cheese onto each wrapper. Brush the edges of the wrappers with a little beaten egg. Place another wrapper on top, and ensure that the edges are well sealed.

Dice the mushrooms and *foie gras*. Sauté the *foie gras* over a high flame. Add the mushrooms and continue to sauté in the fat produced. Season and arrange on a plate.

Presentation: Boil the *wonton ravioli* for about five to seven minutes and drain. Spoon into a deep dish. Decorate with the sautéed *foie gras* and mushrooms. Drizzle with white truffle oil and garnish with tarragon leaves.

Gambas con chorizo y salsa de guanábana
Prawns with *chorizo* sausage and guanábana (soursop) sauce

Wilo Benet

Serves 4
4 prawns
450g chorizo *sausage (smoked pork sausage)*
170g butter
170g soursop or prickly custard apple purée
2 shallots chopped
60g rice vinegar
60g white wine
60g double cream
Chives
Olive oil
Salt
Pepper

Prepare the sauce in a medium-sized pan. Melt 30g of butter over a low heat and sauté the chopped shallots until they are soft and translucent. Now add the vinegar and white wine. Leave the liquid to reduce by half. Add the cream. Leave to boil for two minutes, add the mashed soursop pulp and boil for a further two minutes. Remove the pan from the heat and beat vigorously with a whisk. Now add the remaining butter. Season.

Cut the *chorizo* sausage into julienne strips, brown in a frying pan in its own fat. Place into a warm oven to keep hot. Peel the prawns, leaving the tails intact. Make an incision in the meat. Brown both sides of the prawns in olive oil in a griddle pan. Cook until crispy (between three and four minutes).

Presentation: Spoon a little fried *chorizo* onto a plate. Delicately place a prawn on top. Drizzle the sauce around the prawn and decorate with chives.

Foie gras *a la plancha con plátanos maduros*
Grilled *foie gras* with yellow plantains

Wilo Benet

Serves 4
240g foie gras
4 tablespoons truffle honey
2 yellow plantains
120g coriander
Flour
Vegetable oil
Salt
Pepper

First, cut the *foie gras* into slices, season, coat in flour and place into the fridge. Cut the plantains into approximately 21/2 centimetre slices. Fry in vegetable oil until golden. Drain on absorbent kitchen paper and keep hot.

Place the *foie gras* under a very hot grill and cook until both sides are crispy and golden brown.

Presentation: Arrange the *foie gras* on top of the plantains, drizzle the truffle honey around the edges of the plate and garnish with coriander.

Potaje de yautía con crujiente de serrano

Mario Pagán | ## Cream of taro root with crispy ham

Serves 4

800g taro root (yautía)
150g dry cured ham (jamón Serrano)
100g onion sliced
1 garlic clove sliced
4 cups chicken stock
Salt

Peel and chop the taro root. Heat the chicken stock in a pan. When it starts to boil, add the taro root, and the onion and garlic clove to flavour the stock. Cook until tender. Now pulse in a blender until creamy. Add salt and more chicken stock if necessary.

Cut the ham into fine strips. Fry in oil until golden and crispy. Serve in soup bowls. Decorate with a small handful of crispy ham strips.

Mario Pagán

Vieira con corteza de bacalao envuelta en ajo puerro sobre puré de batata local y crema de maíz con trufa

Scallop with cod paste wrapped in leek, served on a bed of sweet potato purée and drizzled in cream of sweetcorn with truffle

Serves 4

4 scallops
2 sweet potatoes
120g cod, desalted & poached
80g leek
60g coconut milk
Salt

For the cream of sweetcorn with truffle:
100g sweetcorn kernels
225g double cream
2 shallots
15g truffle
Salt

Peel and chop the sweet potatoes. Cook for fifteen minutes in boiling water. Drain and mash to form a purée. Season to taste and mix with the coconut milk. Set aside.

Fry the scallops until golden brown. Now place into a 200°C oven for four minutes.

Mash the cod to a paste. Finely slice the leek and sauté.

For the cream of sweetcorn with truffle: Place the cream, sweetcorn and shallots in a pan. Leave to cook over a low heat for fifteen minutes, until the sweetcorn is tender. Pulse in a blender and then press through a sieve or mouli to obtain the cream. Return the cream to the pan and leave to reduce for eight minutes. Add grated truffle and salt to taste.

Presentation: Stuff a circular slice of leek with a scallop and cover with the mashed cod paste. Place on a bed of sweet potato. Drizzle with the cream of sweetcorn and truffle.

Mario Pagán

Filete de rodaballo atlántico sobre arborio negro, calabaza y rúcula baby del país
Turbot fillet on a layer of black *Arborio* rice with pumpkin and baby rocket

Serves 4
4 200g turbot fillets
500ml vegetable stock
2 cups Arborio risotto rice
100g squid ink
80g pumpkin
Baby rocket
Salt

Fry turbot fillets over a high flame. Transfer to a baking tray and bake for eight minutes at 200°C. Heat the vegetable stock in a pan and add the squid ink.

When the stock starts to boil, add the rice and cook over a medium heat until done. Now drain, reserving the liquid, and set aside. Return the liquid to the heat and reduce until thick.

Dice the pumpkin and cook in boiling water with a pinch of salt. When soft, drain and mix with the black rice. Season with salt and arrange into a mound in the centre of the plate. Remove the turbot from the oven and place immediately on top of the rice. Decorate with baby rocket. Finally, garnish with the black sauce and additional pumpkin.

Douglas Rodríguez

Ceviche arco iris
Rainbow *ceviche*

Serves 4

225g wreck fish, finely sliced
225g salmon, finely sliced
120g tuna, finely diced
4 spring onions, finely chopped
diagonally

For the citrus juice marinade:

1/2 cup of orange juice
1/2 cup lemon juice
1/2 cup soy sauce
2 tablespoons lemon oil
1 tablespoon jalapeno *or spicy*
vinegar
2 tablespoons honey
2 tablespoons fresh grated
ginger
1 teaspoon ground red pepper

For the garnish:

1/2 cup chopped coriander
1/2 red onion, finely chopped
1 tablespoon white sesame
seeds

To make the citrus juice marinade, mix all the ingredients in a bowl. Add the wreck fish and salmon and leave to marinade for two minutes. Soak the tuna in a little soy sauce. Now arrange the marinated wreck fish slices on a dish in a straight line. Place the slices of salmon over the wreck fish and top with the diced tuna. Drizzle with a little citrus juice marinade. To garnish, sprinkle with chopped onion, coriander and toasted sesame seeds.s

Ostras Rodríguez
Rodríguez oysters

Douglas Rodríguez

Douglas Rodríguez

Serves 4

2 1/2 cups creamy milk
2 tablespoons fresh horseradish,
grated
1/2kg fresh spinach
3 tablespoons Manchego or
cured sheep's cheese
Oil

For the breaded oysters:
12 oysters
1 beaten egg
Panko (Japanese breadcrumbs)
Flour

For the purée:
5 boiled yellow plantains
60g streaky or fat bacon
2 finely chopped red onions
Salt
Pepper

Fry the spinach in a dash of oil until soft. In another frying pan, fry the horseradish until it has reduced by half. Place into a bowl. Add the grated *Manchego* cheese and the creamy milk. Now add the spinach and cook together for a few minutes. Set aside.

For the purée: Fry the chopped bacon and finely chopped onion. Boil the plantains, drain and mash to a purée. Add to the frying pan when the onion is golden. Lightly sauté and season. Set aside.

For the oysters: Open the oysters and remove the shells. Coat each oyster in flour, egg and panko. Fry in plenty of oil at 160°C until golden.

Presentation: Spoon a tablespoon of purée into each shell (three shells per person), place the spinach cream on top and crown with the breaded oyster.

Douglas Rodríguez

Brazo de gitano de dulce de leche
Caramelised Swiss roll

Serves 4
For the sponge:
6 eggs
180g granulated sugar
90g flour
4 teaspoons vanilla extract
Whipped cream

For the caramelised condensed milk:
250 ml whole milk
2 teaspoons vanilla extract
4 cups sugar

For the iced soursop
900g fresh soursop (or prickly custard apple) pulp
1 cup sugar
2 cups water

For the condensed milk: Place the milk, sugar and vanilla in a pan, stir well and leave to cook for between 2 1/2 to 3 hours, stirring occasionally until thick. Leave the caramelised condensed milk to cool overnight.

For the iced soursop: Heat the water and sugar over the heat until it dissolves. Leave to stand at room temperature. When lukewarm, add the soursop pulp. Mix well and place in the fridge for at least six hours.

The sponge: Pre-heat the oven to 170°C. Beat the egg yolks with the sugar and the vanilla extract until creamy. Beat the egg whites until stiff and then fold into the egg yolk mixture little by little. Sift the flour into the mixture, fold, and pour into a greased baking tray. Bake for eight to ten minutes. When it has cooled, remove from the tin and cut it into a rectangle. Spread with caramelised condensed milk and roll up. Completely cover with whipped cream and place in fridge until ready for serving.

Presentation: Cut the Swiss roll into portions. Spoon the iced soursop onto a plate, and carefully place a portion of Swiss roll on top. Decorate with slices of fresh ripe mango.

Drinks

Without doubt, rum is the most popular alcoholic drink in most Caribbean countries. The larger islands have their own brands of rum, which is used as a base for many cocktails including *Cuba libre, piña colada, daiquiri* and *mojito,* drinks that have become extremely popular throughout the world. The people of the Caribbean also take advantage of excellent indigenous tropical fruits to make juices and sorbets.

Rum is a distillation obtained from the juice or molasses of sugar cane that has been fermented to obtain alcohol. Its origins date back to 1493 when Christopher Columbus introduced sugar cane cultivation onto the island of La Española – which later became Haiti and the Dominican Republic. From its early beginnings, sugar cane cultivation quickly spread outwards to other areas of the Caribbean. It would not be long before it was discovered that by-products of the sugar production process fermented into alcohol. Later, distillation of these by-products concentrated the alcohol and removed impurities, producing the first true rums. The first written evidence of this distillation dates back to around 1650 in Barbados. At the time, a very strong spirit was made, which was named *rumbullion* (also known as kill devil) a word that was used to refer to a great riot or fight, and that would later become the root of the present-day name of the drink: rum.

Over the next few centuries, rum earned a reputation as being the drink of sailors and pirates as it helped maintain spirits during long sea voyages. In the Caribbean, rum production became important economically and socially, firstly due to the arrival of African slaves who worked in the sugar cane plantations, a group of peoples who considerably influenced the culture of the islands. In the 17th and 18th centuries, rum was also used as a currency for trading slaves and for commerce.

The demand for rum increased substantially, so much so, that distilleries were built in New England and New York to increase supply, and molasses were sent over from the Caribbean. From that moment on, production levels have continued to grow and rum is now considered one of the most popular alcoholic drinks in the world today. On the islands of Cuba, Puerto Rico, Jamaica, Dominican Republic and Barbados, a number of distilleries still survive, producing well-known brands that are popular throughout the world.

Rum cocktails

Depending on the process and length of distillation, rum may vary from being colourless to golden or dark brown, and it may be infused with fruit extracts or spices.

In the Caribbean, the strongest and tastiest rums of all come from Jamaica, and are often diluted in a lemon or fruit-juice punch. Most Caribbean countries still traditionally drink rum neat or with ice, while elsewhere, rum is often used as a base for many well-known cocktails, whose origins are full of curious facts, and occasionally, contradictions.

For example, the classic cocktail *Cuba libre*, made with rum, coca cola and a slice of lemon, was created during the war between Spain and North America at the end of the 19th century. The world-famous Bacardi brand tells us how an American officer asked for a drink with rum, coca-cola and lime juice in a bar in Havana. The combination was an immediate success and one of the soldiers toasted "*una Cuba libre*" (free Cuba). The origin of *daiquiri* – a cocktail made with white rum, lemon juice, a few drops of maraschino, sugar and crushed ice, can be also dated to the Cuban war of Independence, although some people claim the drink was 'invented' by an American general; others dispute this fact, claiming that the real inventor was an engineer who worked in the mines in Daiquiri, a small town. Yet both stories claim that ice was added to the simple combination of rum and lemon. The cocktail was immortalised by the writer Ernest Hemingway, who asked for it in El Floridita bar in Havana's old central district. The *mojito,* made in a tumbler, with sugar, mint leaves, lime and lemon juice, soda water and rum, is drunk through a straw. It was created at the start of the 1930s when Cuban hotels wished to offer a new drink to American tourists, at a time when alcohol was banned in America. Less potent than *daiquiri, mojito*

can be drunk at any time of the day. *Piña colada,* made with coconut cream, pineapple juice and white rum, was created in Puerto Rico in the mid-1950s. It was founded by a barman called Ramón Marrero, known as "Monchito", who worked at the Caribe Milton Hotel. He experimented with several alcoholic combinations that would prevent his customers from having their daily hangovers. In Puerto Rico, where a large part of the rum that is exported to America is produced, the following drinks are also popular: *rum sangria*, which is made by adding pieces of apple and grapes, and *mai tai,* made with lemon juice, orange juice, almond syrup, grenadine, golden rum and dark rum.

Other drinks

Despite the overwhelming predominance of rum, Caribbean countries also produce other interesting drinks from their incredible supply of local tropical fruits and plants.

In Cuba, *guarapo,* a sugar cane juice with African roots, is served with a little ice, and *pru*, made from roots, is also popular. It is also good for the digestive system. In the Dominican Republic, *pru* is known as *mabí* and is also served very cold. In addition, *cacheo* is also popular in the country. It is made by briefly fermenting the molasses from the stem of a palm tree – also known as *cacheo.* Coffee liqueur has become popular around the world, thanks to the success of Tía María, the Jamaican coffee liqueur, also used in cocktails.

Coffee is also extremely popular in Cuba and Puerto Rico, where it is drunk in small amounts and is highly concentrated. Natural juices such as Cuban lemonade, tamarind, pineapple, papaya, guava and mango juice are especially popular. Milkshakes are also common, and are made with pieces of fruit, sugar and a little milk. They can be served as a drink or drunk for dessert. As in other parts of the world, beer is also popular, and Cuban branded beers are widely drunk throughout the Caribbean.

Index

The Times World Cook Books

Complete 20 exclusive volumes of a unique collection

South America

Caribbean Islands

China

United States of America

Scandinavia

France (I)

France (II)

Greece

India (I)

India (II)

Italy (II)

Japan

Mexico

Morocco

Portugal

Thailand (I)

Thailand (II)

United Kingdom

Spain

Italy (I)

The Times World Cook Book Collection Offer (120 Page Full Colour volumes)

Title	Available for purchase from:	Price (inc P&P)	Quantity	Total (£)
Italy I (60pp Sampler)	29-Oct-2005	£1.99		
Italy II	05-Nov 2005	£3.98		
Morocco	12-Nov 2005	£3.98		
USA	19-Nov 2005	£3.98		
India I	26-Nov 2005	£3.98		
Japan	03-Dec 2005	£3.98		
South America	10-Dec 2005	£3.98		
Thailand I	17-Dec 2005	£3.98		
Portugal	24-Dec 2005	£3.98		
Caribbean	31-Dec 2006	£3.98		
Scandinavia	07-Jan 2006	£3.98		
India II	14-Jan 2006	£3.98		
Greece	21-Jan 2006	£3.98		
France I	28-Jan 2006	£3.98		
Thailand II	04-Feb 2006	£3.98		
UK	11-Feb 2006	£3.98		
China	18-Feb 2006	£3.98		
France II	25-Feb 2006	£3.98		
Mexico	04-Mar 2006	£3.98		
Spain	11-Mar 2006	£3.98		
Full Set *	(20% discount)	£59.99		
		Total Price		**£**

* Readers who subscribe to the Full Set will be sent a book each week until the collection is complete.
Please send 10 mastheads of any The Times or Sunday Times with each Full Set ordered.

Title: _____ Initial: _____ Surname: _____

Address: _____

_____

Postcode: _____ DOB: _____ / _____ / _____

Phone # : _____ Email: _____ @ _____

I enclose a cheque/PO made payable to 'Times Cookery Books Offer', and a newspaper masthead (Times logo) for each book I've ordered. Price above includes postage and packing.
Send to **"Times Cookery Books Offer", PO Box 142, Horsham RH13 5FJ.** Please allow 28 days for delivery.

For the sum of **£** ....
Or please debit my Visa / Mastercard / Maestro for **£** ....
Card Number _____
Issue date (maestro only) ...... / ....
Start Date .... / .... Close Date .... / ....

Signature _____